I0795397

IMAGES
of America

POP WARNER LITTLE SCHOLARS

Pop Warner Little Scholars has always placed a strong emphasis on education, culture, and experience. In the early years of the Scholar All-American program, winners were often rewarded with trips to various locations across the country. Frequently, these scholar-athletes would have the opportunity to visit and explore the history-rich culture of Philadelphia. One of the most popular attractions in Philadelphia even today is the Liberty Bell, one of the nation's oldest symbols of freedom.

IMAGES
of America

POP WARNER LITTLE SCHOLARS

Joel D. Balthaser

ARCADIA

ISBN 0-7385-3505-2

First published 2004

Published by Arcadia Publishing,
an imprint of Tempus Publishing Inc.
Portsmouth NH, Charleston SC, Chicago,
San Francisco

Printed in Great Britain

Library of Congress Catalog Card Number: 2003114950

For all general information, contact Arcadia Publishing:
Telephone 843-853-2070
Fax 843-853-0044
E-mail sales@arcadiapublishing.com
For customer service and orders:
Toll-free 1-888-313-2665

Visit us on the Internet at www.arcadiapublishing.com

In the years following World War I, the focus on Pop Warner participants was shifted to a younger generation, primarily ages 15 and under. At this time, one of the strongest programs was Sheriff Austin Meehan's Philadelphia Moose Clickets, a team of 13- and 14-year-olds. Pictured is the starting backfield of the 115-pound champion Clickets of 1949. The boys are, from left to right, running back Dick Stultz (No. 34), fullback Buckie Keane (No. 22), running back Howard Ogden (No. 6), and quarterback John Kelly (No. 21).

Contents

Legendary football coach Glenn S. Warner, better known as "Pop" Warner, was the only invited guest to make it to a spring clinic held by the five-year-old Junior Football Conference in Philadelphia in 1934. Battling his way through snow and ice, Warner showed up for the clinic and spent the next several hours talking with some 800 youths attending the event. The participants and coaches of the program were in awe of the generosity and character of Warner and voted unanimously to rename the program the Pop Warner Conference. Pop Warner went on to play a major role in the organization's success until his death in 1954.

INTRODUCTION

Pop Warner Hall of Fame member and legendary football coach Vince Lombardi once said, "The spirit, the will to win, and the will to excel are the things that endure. These qualities are so much more important than the events that occur." Back in 1929, founder Joseph Tomlin organized a youth football conference with very similar principles. Although he had no idea of the impact it would have on America, Tomlin had a vision of an organization that would provide youths with an organized sports team while shaping them into well-rounded individuals.

Started in the suburbs of Philadelphia during the early years of the Great Depression, the Junior Football Conference was established as a four-team league with just a few players. After just a few seasons, it was quickly renamed in honor of legendary football coach Glenn S. "Pop" Warner, a name that brought the organization immediate popularity. The Pop Warner Conference quickly expanded into a national and, eventually, an international organization behind the commitment of Tomlin and his peers. "Individual commitment to a group effort, that is what makes a team work, a company work, a society work, a civilization work," Lombardi often proclaimed.

The history of Pop Warner goes much deeper than just football and cheerleading, however. Mandatory academic requirements, a uniform set of rules, as well as an annual national championship and scholastic recognition program have set Pop Warner apart from other youth sports organizations for several years. Encouraging youth participation, ensuring a safe and positive environment, and instilling lifelong values into each participant is what Pop Warner is all about. Buffalo Bills quarterback Drew Bledsoe stated, "What Pop Warner is doing for the betterment of children is a step in the right direction for helping develop our leaders of tomorrow."

This book illustrates the history of the largest national youth football and cheerleading organization in the country and highlights the major factors that contributed to the success of Pop Warner. Included in these chapters are the conference's beginnings, football greats Warner and Tomlin, the excitement of the Golden Anniversary Dinner, and the key programs that embody Pop Warner Little Scholars. This is the history of 75 years of Pop Warner Little Scholars, the organization once described as "organized juvenile sports at its best."

Emmitt Smith, the 1996 Pop Warner Inspiration to Youth Award recipient, stated, "When I played Pop Warner football, I had a great deal of fun. You could be a kid, you could run around, you could laugh, you could holler. Those were great moments."

One

The Beginning Years: 1929–1959

In 1929, the owner of the Horace T. Potts Company building in Northeast Philadelphia was faced with a huge problem. His factory's large windows were constantly being broken by teenagers throwing stones at them from a nearby lot. After nearly 100 windows were broken in just one month, the building's owner called upon the help of his friend Joseph J. Tomlin to help solve the recurring problem.

Joseph Tomlin, a sports enthusiast and revered athlete, had a possible answer. Since the other factories in the area were also being plagued by the young vandals, he suggested that Horace Potts and other building owners get together to fund an athletic program for the youngsters. In those days, the city did not have organized recreation programs to keep idle children occupied and out of trouble. The owners quickly agreed to help fund the new organization, and Tomlin began crafting ideas for a new athletic program.

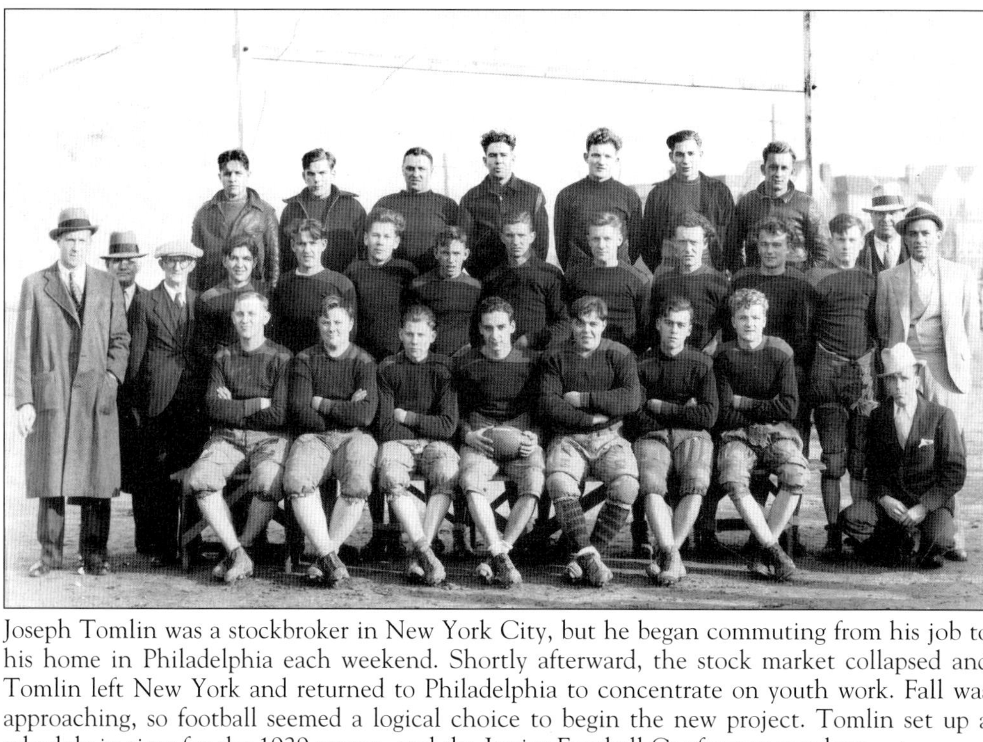

Joseph Tomlin was a stockbroker in New York City, but he began commuting from his job to his home in Philadelphia each weekend. Shortly afterward, the stock market collapsed and Tomlin left New York and returned to Philadelphia to concentrate on youth work. Fall was approaching, so football seemed a logical choice to begin the new project. Tomlin set up a schedule in time for the 1929 season, and the Junior Football Conference was born.

Comprised of just four teams, the Junior Football Conference's main goal was to assist the Philadelphia Chamber of Commerce in controlling the behaviors of teenaged children. However, Joseph Tomlin believed it could help with much more than that. He emphasized the importance of education and began to shape the young men into gentlemen. Behind this philosophy, the Junior Football Conference quickly expanded to 16 teams by 1933.

Young Junior Football Conference participants received tips and techniques about the game of football from many different sources. With football being played at this time primarily by much older players, these young students of the game were eager to learn. Here, two referees educate a young participant on the proper way to kick the ball, as his teammate attentively looks on.

Player registrations for Pop Warner teams where often held at central locations of the cities, convenient to all neighborhoods. Shown is one of these locations in downtown Philadelphia, on the corner of Delaware Avenue and Market Street. Players would await their turn in long lines to complete the registration process of signing up, being weighed, and posing for a photograph. Although the process is more complex today, the basic requirements remain the same.

On April 19, 1934, the Junior Football Conference had a spring clinic for its teams and was scheduled to have several local college coaches speak to the 800 young football players attending. However, a storm hit the area that night and only one coach showed up, Glenn Scobie "Pop" Warner. Warner, who had just arrived in Philadelphia to begin coaching for the Temple Owls, spent several hours answering questions and speaking with the excited youths. At the end of the evening, the participants were so delighted that they voted and unanimously decided to rename the program the Pop Warner Conference.

With the new prestigious Pop Warner name, the conference grew tremendously over the next several years. By 1938, a total of 157 teams were competing, mostly based upon weight. They were fielded against opponents of similar size. Although the vast majority of players were age 15 or so, a few participants were as old as 30. The original teams represented neighborhoods in the city, and the newer suburban teams represented towns.

Pictured here are the members of the 1937 Benner Athletic Association football team, one of the first organizations established in the conference. Here, head coach Robert Peacock (front row, far left) and his players pose for their annual team picture. They are dressed in formal attire, as always, before a quarter-final match-up against Fairmount of Washington, D.C. The previous year, Benner went undefeated and won the senior championship division of the Pop Warner Conference.

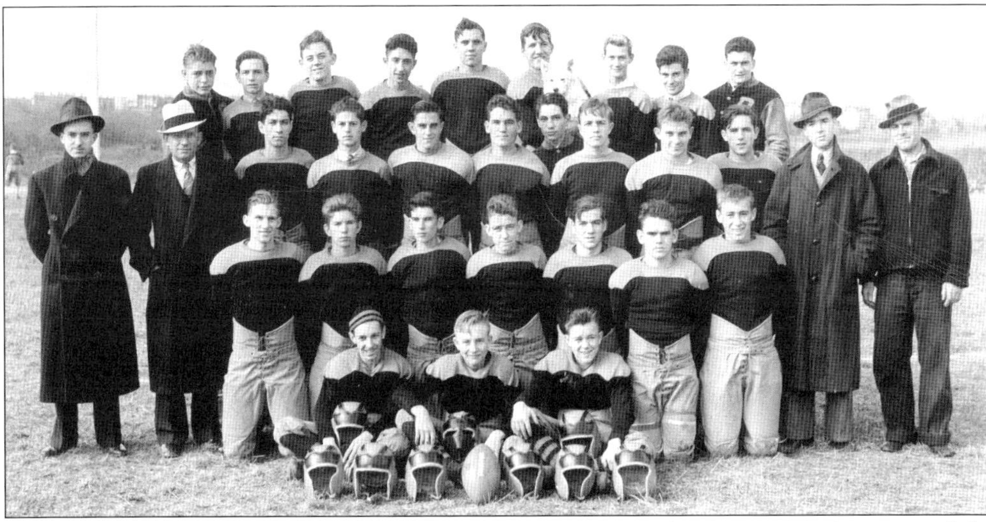

Even in the early years, teams and players were honored for their sportsmanship, one of the main benefits of being a member of the Pop Warner Conference. In 1937, the Holmesburg Ramblers (above) were honored for displaying the best sportsmanship throughout the season. What also made this team unique was that most of the players had participated in the same program for almost 13 years together, including prior to joining the Junior Football Conference.

During the years of the Great Depression (1929–1939), poverty forced a large number of youngsters to leave school. Joseph Tomlin, a great believer in the importance of education, fought the trend by supplying the youths with books and arranging for them to hear guest speakers. He also recruited tutors for "marginal" youngsters who wanted to stay in school. This commitment to the principles of scholastic aptitude has always been an integral part of the Pop Warner program.

Just when the program began gaining tremendous increases in participation, World War II began and the Pop Warner Conference lost most of its older players. Several of its participants enlisted in the military and many squads began to fold, while others merged with other programs in order to have enough players to compete. By the end of 1940, only 42 teams remained.

The end of the war came in 1946, and although the Pop Warner Conference rebounded to 100 teams for the 1947 season, there was a shift in membership. Many of the returning servicemen had abandoned playing football altogether. The new programs, organized for youngsters aged 15 and under, divided participants into groups based on ages and weights. Divisions such as Pee Wees and Midgets were established as a result of the new safety rules.

As new programs with younger participants began to emerge, so did cheerleading. Teams were often encouraged to have a staff of girl cheerleaders with them for their games. Although a cheerleading program was not officially recognized until 1967, cheerleaders have always been an important part of the games and have been included in national scholastic recognition.

In the early 1940s, the Pop Warner Conference drafted a character code that embodied the program and its participants. The seven principles were self-reliance (do the job yourself), self-control (keep a cool head), self-respect (your word, your bond), respect of property (vandalism is stealing), respect of leadership (your coach knows best), respect of others (sell nobody short), and competitive spirit (fight to the very end).

Frank Palumbo was a major contributor to the Pop Warner Conference. Palumbo, who owned three restaurants in the Philadelphia area, often hosted various Pop Warner Conference meetings and All-Conference team dinners, usually paying for them himself. In 1947, Palumbo had an idea of a bowl game that would feature the champion of the Pop Warner Conference versus an outside team. Palumbo called upon the help of his good friend Frank Sinatra to sponsor the visiting team.

On December 27, 1947, Joseph Tomlin organized the first major championship game in the organization's young history. Sponsored by the *Philadelphia Daily News*, the Santa Claus Bowl was played in six inches of snow before 2,000 spectators at South Philadelphia High School. A Philadelphia Midget team called Palumbo's Clickets, named after Palumbo's Philadelphia supper club, played Sinatra's Cyclones, a New York team sponsored by musician Frank Sinatra. The Palumbo's Clickets won the game, 6-0, and the Pop Warner Conference won the attention of the nation for the first time.

The 1947 Santa Claus Bowl was one of the first noncollegiate bowl games ever played. Each year, the event drew more attention, and it expanded to locations such as Lynchburg and Roanoke, Virginia; Lakeland, Florida; and Omaha, Nebraska. The annual event also encouraged a series of other annual bowl games, including the Kids Army-Navy Game, the Toys for Tots Bowl, and the Piggy Bank Bowl.

This 1949 photograph shows the Pennypack Midgets visiting the Venango Midgets at UGI Field in Northeast Philadelphia. The uniforms of the Pennypack players were typical of the times, and helmets were shared between offensive and defensive players. Sidelines were often constructed of objects similar to the fire hose used at this game, as fields were typically only lined properly for the older-division games, which took place on Saturdays.

In the 1949 Santa Claus Bowl, the Yeadon Boys Club of Philadelphia traveled to Omaha to play a dairy-sponsored squad called Robert's Pure Paks. Coach Andy Reeder's squad (above) had a difficult time matching up against the new program and lost the game 46-0.

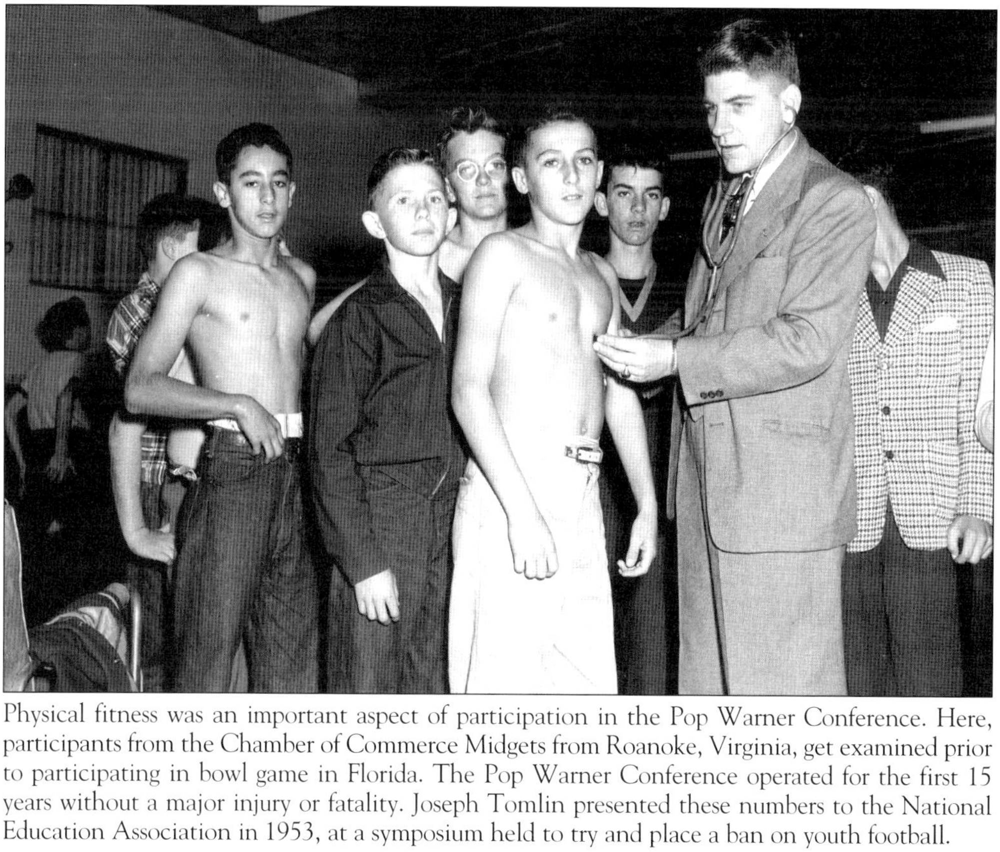

Physical fitness was an important aspect of participation in the Pop Warner Conference. Here, participants from the Chamber of Commerce Midgets from Roanoke, Virginia, get examined prior to participating in bowl game in Florida. The Pop Warner Conference operated for the first 15 years without a major injury or fatality. Joseph Tomlin presented these numbers to the National Education Association in 1953, at a symposium held to try and place a ban on youth football.

In 1956, the Pop Warner Conference took a bold step when it decided to become exclusively a Midget football association. New rules were drafted, and the program allowed only boys age 16 and under to participate, with an emphasis beginning at 13 years old and under. Although these rules were established nearly 50 years ago, the organization continues to operate with a similar structure today.

By the end of the 1958 season, the Pop Warner Conference had expanded from the East Coast all the way to the West Coast in California. The Pop Warner Board met later that year and decided it was time to take the program to the national level. With Joseph Tomlin's business now prospering, he had more time to devote to the program. By the start of the 1959 football season, Tomlin's unimaginable dream of a national football program was now a reality, as the Pop Warner Conference was officially incorporated as Pop Warner Little Scholars Inc., a name chosen unanimously to reflect the equal importance of academics and athletics.

Red Smith, a legendary sportswriter, once wrote, "Pop Warner was a gruff old gent, kind and forthright and obstinate and honest. He was one of the few truly original minds in football coaching, and that made him a big man in his world. There is, however, a more important measure of a football coach than his contribution to and influence on the technique of the game. The quality of the man himself is revealed in the attitude of his former players after they have outgrown the awed hero worship of undergraduate days. After the boys who played for him had become men, Pop remained a hero to them."

Two

Glenn S. "Pop" Warner

Glenn Scobie "Pop" Warner coached football from 1895 until 1938. In his 44 years as a coach, he compiled an incredible record of 341-118-33, won 4 national championships, and produced 30 All-America players. To date, Warner is the seventh-winningest coach in college football history. However, he was more interested in the character-building aspects of football than in the numbers. "The youth who doesn't thrill to the strain of struggle and the joy of victory isn't much of a lad," declared Warner.

Glenn Warner was born in upstate New York in a farmhouse (now known as Nunweiler's Corners) just outside of Springville in 1871. After graduating from the Griffith Institute in 1889, he moved with his family to Wichita Falls, Texas, where he worked as a tinsmith for three years. In the summer of 1892, Warner returned to Springville for a summer vacation and to play his favorite sport, baseball. That summer in Springville, Warner had the opportunity to play against baseball great John McGraw.

BIG CHIEF POP WARNER.

Following his summer vacation, Glenn Warner began to spend his time following the Grand Circuit harness races, making wagers along the way. However, after he had lost all of his money at a race in Rochester, he wrote to his father back in Texas of his interest in attending law school at Cornell University. Very interested in having him become a lawyer, his father sent him enough money ($100) to enroll at Cornell.

As a freshman, Glenn Warner thought his sports career would begin on the baseball team. However, when Warner met the captain of the Cornell football team, Carl Johanson, on a train to Ithaca, he was quickly persuaded to pursue a career on the football field due to his size. At the time, Warner weighed over 200 pounds but had never played football. "Up to that time I had only seen the game of football, but had not thought of ever trying to play it," Warner later proclaimed.

The game came naturally to Glenn Warner, who was later named captain of the football team. As a freshman, Warner earned the name "Pop" because, at age 22, he was much older than most of his teammates. Later, his brother Bill was nicknamed "Young Pop." Warner was not only a great football player at Cornell but also excelled in track and field and was the college's heavyweight boxing champion in 1893, defeating a two-year reigning champion.

After graduating from Cornell in 1895, Pop Warner began practicing law in Buffalo. A few months later, he accepted a position at Iowa State, where for $25 a week, he helped the football team condition and prepare for the upcoming season. He also agreed to coach the University of Georgia for the remaining few months of their season. Thus, at the same time, he helped coach two different university teams in two different states.

In 1895, the University of Georgia hired Pop Warner as its new football coach at a salary of $340 for 10 weeks. He arrived in Athens, Georgia, on September 15, 1895, homesick and discouraged after seeing the sports facilities and staff at his disposal. At the time, the University of Georgia had no athletic facilities, playing field, or stands. In fact, the only place for playing football or any other sport was a bare field behind New College, where rocks stuck out of the red clay. In 1895, the University of Georgia's entire student body consisted of just 248 students, and only 13 of those showed up to play football. As a result, Warner's first team, the 1895 squad, had only three wins with four losses. Warner was rehired for the 1896 season at a salary of $40 per week. Warner's last Georgia team went 4-0, giving the University of Georgia its first undefeated season.

Pop Warner returned to Cornell to accept an offer of $800 for the next football season. In the five years that he spent coaching for Cornell, Warner posted an impressive 36-13-3 record, including a 10-2 season in 1898, when his team outscored its opponents by 267 points.

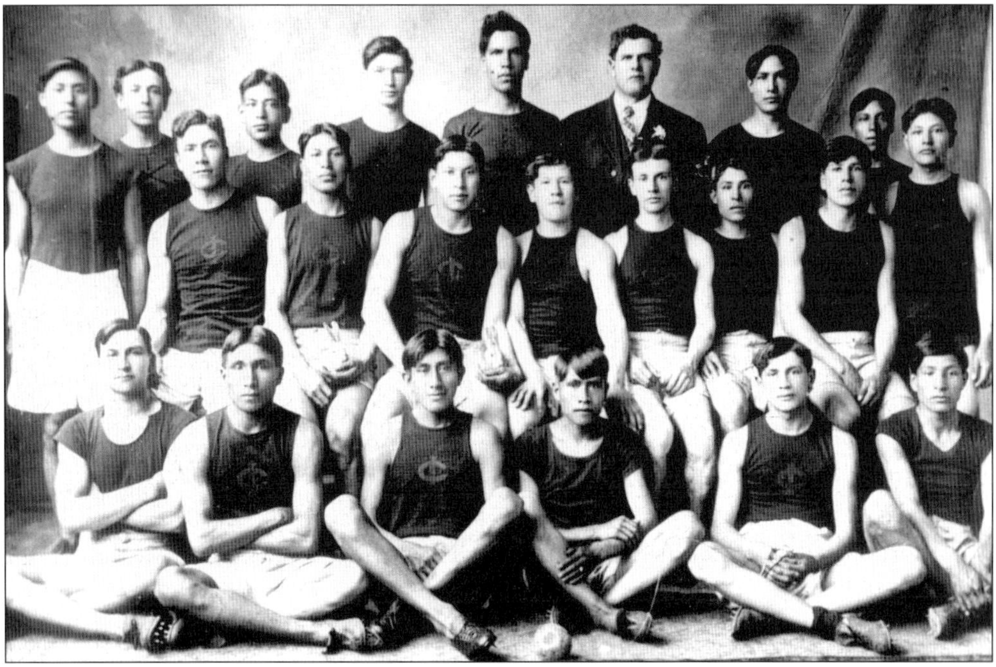

Pop Warner's next job landed him in Carlisle at the Carlisle Indian Industrial School. At Carlisle, Warner served as athletic director and the baseball, track, boxing, and head football coach. With Warner at the helm, Carlisle was quickly transformed into a major national championship–contending school. In the 15-year span from 1899 to 1914, Warner coached 12 seasons at Carlisle, posting an impressive 114-42-8 record.

While at Carlisle, Pop Warner tutored several great athletes in sports history, including Chief Bender, Jim Thorpe, and Louis Tewanima. Here, Warner meets with Olympic greats Louis Tewanima and Jim Thorpe prior to their departure for the 1912 Olympics in Stockholm, Sweden. Tewanima won Olympic medals in 1908 and 1912; Thorpe won the decathlon and pentathlon events at the 1912 Olympics.

Pop Warner helped train Jim Thorpe prior to the 1912 Olympics, and he was known for his innovations and commitment to training and preparation. One biographer claimed, "Warner was a trailblazer who led football out of the wilderness of masses, closed-order, push-pull and huddle into the open game of speed, deception and brains."

Pop Warner was blessed with the remarkable young halfback named Jim Thorpe. Warner helped convert Thorpe into one of the greatest rushers, passers, and kickers of all time. In what may have been his most remarkable season as a head coach, Warner won a national championship with Carlisle. Thorpe scored 25 touchdowns and 198 points in leading his Carlisle Indian School team to a national collegiate championship that year.

At the summer Olympics of 1912 in Stockholm, Sweden, young Jim Thorpe turned in an incredible performance. His dominance in track and field resulted in a fourth-place finish in the high jump, a seventh-place finish in the long jump, and the gold medals in the pentathlon and decathlon events. Pop Warner soon after declared Jim Thorpe "the greatest all-around athlete in the world."

After the Carlisle Indian School was closed in 1914, Pop Warner moved on to coach at the University of Pittsburgh. He coached for nine seasons, compiling a record of 60-12-4, including four undefeated seasons and national championships in 1915, 1916 (unanimously), and 1918 (unanimously). At one point, his Pittsburgh Panthers won an incredible 33 straight games.

When Pop Warner took the coaching job at Stanford University in 1923, he had no idea he was about to coach another of the greatest college athletes of the 20th century. Ernie Nevers, whom Pop Warner described as someone who "gave everything he had in every game," helped lead Stanford to the 1925 Rose Bowl against Notre Dame and the legendary "four horsemen." Although Stanford lost 27-10, an injured Nevers led all players with 117 yards rushing and an interception on defense. Later in life, Nevers presented awards at the annual Pop Warner awards banquet.

Pop Warner's final head coaching job was one that helped secure his name in football for a long time to come. Warner took the head coaching job at Temple University in 1932 for an unprecedented $75,000 for five seasons with the new program. While coaching in Philadelphia for the Temple Owls, Warner was invited to speak to a clinic of the Junior Football Conference, which shortly thereafter was renamed in his honor. Here, Warner catches up on some sleep before a Temple practice.

Pop Warner is credited with introducing several major innovations to college football such as the spiral punt, the screen play, single and double-wing formations, the naked reverse, the three-point stance, the numbering on players' jerseys, and the use of shoulder and thigh pads. "I consider Warner to be the greatest creative genius in American Football. Most of us coaches are imitators, but Pop Warner was an inventor," said Hall of Fame coach Andy Kerr.

When there was a gathering of the most influential sports figures of the time, Pop Warner was usually one of the invited guests. Here, Warner stands for a photograph with football legend Knute Rockne, George Herman "Babe" Ruth, Christy Walsh, T. A. Jones, and F. H. Yost before the Coachmen's Dinner on November 30, 1925, in New York City.

Pop Warner discusses strategy with assistant coach Wallace Denney during a 1938 Temple University football game. Warner spent more than four decades as a coach and brought many innovations to college football that have not only changed the face of the sport but also endured to the present day. He spent 44 years coaching the game of football and was inducted into the College Football Hall of Fame in 1951.

In the spring of 1953, contributions of $15,000 from Pop Warner and his wife, Tibb Loraine Smith, led to the creation of the Warner Museum. The house was built in 1847 and renovated into the museum thanks to the generous contributions. Officially opened on May 22, 1954 (just a few months before Warner's death), the museum honors the "grand old man of football" for all of his accomplishments. It features many items donated directly from Warner himself, including Indian baskets, trinkets, tools, and a long beaded poncho used by Indian medicine men. Shortly before her death in 1961, Tibb donated money for improvements to the monumental building.

Pop Warner spent the last years of his life in Palo Alto, California, near Stanford University. He finished his coaching career helping Dud De Groot and Bon Winkelman coach at San Jose College. He spent his spare time advising coaches from all across the country, painting landscapes, and designing furniture. Glenn Scobie "Pop" Warner passed away on September 7, 1954, in Palo Alto.

On July 25, 1997, the U.S. Postal Service honored four legendary football coaches—Pop Warner, Bear Bryant, Vince Lombardi, and George Halas—with a commemorative stamp. First-day-of-issue ceremonies were held at the Professional Football Hall of Fame in Canton, Ohio. Each stamp was subsequently issued with a red bar above the coach's name in the state most associated with that stamp. On August 8, 1997, the second version of the Pop Warner stamp was issued at LaSalle University in Pennsylvania, the state in which Warner coached for 20 years.

The Warner Award, a tribute to the legendary coach and football icon, was established in 1982 by the board of directors of Pop Warner to honor "the person who has achieved academic excellence in athletics, scholarship and life's endeavors, with integrity and humanity." The award, a to-scale bust of Pop Warner, has been given out for nearly 25 years in remembrance. Well-known CBS-TV sports personality and former Pop Warner trustee chairman Irv Cross received the first award in 1982. Other prominent figures including Joseph Tomlin, Joe Robbie, Ross Perot, Eddie Robinson, and Dick Butkus have also received this distinguished award.

Joseph J. Tomlin was born of immigrant parents on October 19, 1902, in the coal-mining town of Shenandoah. When the boy was just six years old, his father passed away, and he and his mother relocated to Philadelphia to be closer to her family. For most of his younger days he was a standout soccer player, until one day a high-school football coach told him he was "too big for soccer, which was a game for small guys, and that he should play football." The 190-pound freshman started on the varsity team that year and led a great high-school career as a tackle.

Three

JOSEPH J. TOMLIN

Joseph Tomlin decided to attend Gettysburg College but soon after transferred to Swarthmore College, near his home in Philadelphia. A football star at Swarthmore, he graduated with honors in 1927 and went on to study law at Harvard Law School. After one year, Tomlin realized that law was not meant to be his career and began preparations for what would become the Junior Football Conference.

In 1937, Joseph Tomlin founded the Connie Mack Baseball Conference in the greater Philadelphia area. Named after the owner of the old Philadelphia Athletics professional baseball club, the conference gave Tomlin work when the Junior Football Conference was out of season. Although the program took off in the same way that the Junior Football Conference did, Tomlin was forced to step down shortly after World War II, when he could no longer devote his time to two sports. The following year, after forming the Connie Mack Baseball Conference, Tomlin and others helped start the Sandlot Sports Association as a fundraising umbrella for the two programs.

Since the inception of the Junior Football Conference in 1929, Joseph Tomlin had visions of expanding the program across the country and establishing new leagues, even in areas where football was rarely played at that time. One of these places was Hawaii, and in 1946, Tomlin and members of a local Philadelphia team boarded a plane in Washington, D.C., en route to Honolulu to play against the first team in Hawaii. This was just the beginning of Tomlin's dream. The conference began expanding quickly beginning in the early 1950s.

Joseph Tomlin was a true football man, but he also valued the importance of education and made sure his organization extended into the classroom. Even as early as the first few years of the conference, Tomlin supplied his participants with literature and would arrange for them to hear various speakers. This passion for the game was recognized in 1955, when the American Football Coaches Association presented him with the Amos Alonzo Stagg Award, the first time this prestigious award had been presented to a person who was not a college football coach.

In 1965, Frankford High School honored its 1923 graduate Joseph Tomlin with the Pioneer Achievement Award, given to graduates who "do FHS proud" in the course of their life's endeavors. In the nearly 25 years after receiving the award, Tomlin never missed the yearly assembly at his alma mater. Here, Tomlin stops for a picture with fellow Frankford High School alumnus Joe Scott.

Of the many different aspects that he brought to Pop Warner football, Joseph Tomlin claimed that one of his favorite things to do was to hold coaches clinics. Pictured are the participants of the sixth annual Pop Warner Football Coaches Free Clinics, held on July 22, 1971, at the Peddie School in Hightstown, New Jersey. The clinic attracted 102 coaches, who learned about the principle factors of safety in sports, a major aspect of Pop Warner football.

BITS 'N' PIECES

Connecticut Declares Pop Warner Week

Connecticut Governor Ella Grasso, in an official statement, designated the week of November 17-24, 1975 as Pop Warner Super Bowl III Week in Connecticut. She remarked on the important part Pop Warner football plays in the character development of its players, emphasizing such qualities as good sportsmanship, fair play and leadership. Mentioning that **Stamford** would for the third straight year host eight teams in the Connecticut Pop Warner Super Bowl, Governor Grasso saluted the ". . . organizations, coaches and players who give their time and energy to this worthwhile program." Noteworthy among these people is **Jim Hinkle**, Commissioner of the Connecticut Pop Warner Bantam League, who also served this year as Super Bowl III Chairman. Hats off to Connecticut and all Pop Warner people there!

Our thanks to **Les Rose** of Hollister, California who has retired, having served for the past three years as Northern California District Commissioner. He is being replaced by **Sam Lockhart** of Marin County.

Joseph Tomlin was often invited to attend the prestigious awards shows in professional and college football throughout his years. Tomlin was in attendance for the 1975 Heisman Trophy awards dinner in New York City, where he conversed with 1974 Heisman winner Archie Griffin of Ohio State University. Later that evening, Griffin won his second consecutive Heisman Trophy, a feat which has not been equaled to this day.

Joseph Tomlin was a frequent attendee at the Pop Warner national championship even after he stepped away from official business with the company. Here, he is seen enjoying a football game with his good friend Mickey Mouse. In a real honor to the founder, author James Michener stated in his 1976 book, *Sports; A Program for America*, that Pop Warner football was "organized juvenile sports at its best!"

Anyone who knew Joseph Tomlin would describe him as a very passionate person when it came to youth sports but also a very humorous person always up for a laugh. Tomlin shares a laugh with Miami Dolphins legend Don Shula (left), and at the microphone, he greets Oscar Vodgman with a limerick (above).

World heavyweight boxing champion Jack Dempsey was a longtime friend of Joseph Tomlin, as well as a Pop Warner trustee. For several years he worked frequently with Tomlin, sharing wisdom that he had gained over the years and helping to move the program forward. A legendary boxer, Dempsey had a career record of 64-6-9, with 49 of those wins coming by knockout. He was also known for his life after boxing as a successful restaurant owner in New York.

In the second portion of the 1979 golden anniversary banquet, a surprise was in store for Joseph Tomlin. Pop Warner board of directors chairman Leon J. Perelman began the induction of the Pop Warner Hall of Fame by announcing Tomlin as the first to be so honored. Here, Tomlin receives from Perelman a gold football, representing this great accomplishment. In Pop Warner history, only 48 members have been presented with this honor.

In one of his final banquets, Joseph Tomlin was on hand in 1986 to help present the fifth annual Warner Award to H. Ross Perot of Dallas and to induct Ron Jaworski and Dick Vermeil into the Pop Warner Hall of Fame. Here, Tomlin poses for a picture with Perot's sister Bette, who accepted the award that night on her brother's behalf.

Joseph Tomlin helped establish an award to honor those who played key roles in the development of national Pop Warner football. The Old Timer's Award was presented to 13 different individuals and organizations. Here, Tomlin and Liberty Belle Monica Tedori present the award to then Philadelphia Eagles head coach Dick Vermeil for the service and support the National Football League franchise gave to Pop Warner for several years. Dick Vermeil was a longtime friend of Tomlin and supporter of Pop Warner football and cheerleading.

On May 16, 1988, Pop Warner Little Scholars founder Joseph J. Tomlin died at age 85 following a short illness. Nearly 500 people came to pay their respects to this great man who helped shape youth football. Tomlin organized the program in 1929 as a four-team conference in Philadelphia and expanded it into a national and international organization for young boys and girls. At the time of Tomlin's death, Pop Warner football and cheerleading programs had a membership of more than 175,000 boys and girls.

Taking place less than a month after the death of Joseph Tomlin, the 1988 annual dinner was an emotional event. Many people came to honor the true pioneer of youth football, and Philadelphia Mayor Wilson B. Goode began the evening with a very special tribute to Tomlin. This spot in the banquet room was a popular one throughout the night as people came to pay their respects. The previous year at the dinner, Miami Dolphins owner Joe Robbie had introduced Tomlin as "one of the 10 most significant figures in the game of football."

Just one year after Joseph Tomlin's death, the Tomlin Award was created to be given at the annual banquet. This award is presented to an individual who has demonstrated outstanding character development, physical fitness, and academic achievement. The first recipient of the award was Notre Dame Hall of Fame head coach Lou Holtz, who displays his Tomlin Award medallion with pride at the 1989 banquet. The award is still presented today.

Pop Warner national dinner chairman Irv Cross welcomes all of the Little Scholars and their families to Philadelphia for the celebration. Cross, who was well known for his time spent playing for the Philadelphia Eagles or in the broadcast studio for *NFL Today,* is a longtime supporter and frequent attendee of the Pop Warner dinner program. Pop Warner founder and president, Joseph Tomlin, and his son David Tomlin listen attentively from their seats.

Four

The Golden Anniversary Dinner, 1979

Pop Warner celebrated its 50-year anniversary with a gala event at the Philadelphia Marriot on Sunday, May 13, 1979. The two-day event celebrated 50 years of the organization by honoring the 1978 Little Scholars, the top scholastically ranked teams in the country, two volunteers of the year, as well as the 21 All-Time Greats of Football, who were inducted into the inaugural Pop Warner Hall of Fame. This is a view of the ballroom at the Marriott, uniquely decorated for the evening ceremony.

Joseph Tomlin took some time to warm up the crowd as he addressed his remarks to all of the ladies in the audience. The night of the celebration happened to fall on Mother's Day, and Tomlin gave the mothers in attendance due credit to for their hard work and dedication. David Tomlin and Irv Cross enjoy the remarks from Tomlin and share a laugh from the dais.

The dinner banquet of 1979 was the first to which the Little Scholars were invited. Pop Warner chairman of the board Leon Perelman (second from the left) poses for a photograph with Li'l Miss Pop Warner Donna Michelle Loper and her parents. Loper was also the recipient of the scholarship awarded by Perelman, making her trip from Phoenix, Arizona, well worth it. The following day, all of the scholars visited Perelman's Antique Toy Museum, which featured the largest private collection of antique toys in the world.

One of the highlights of the scholar program was the inspirational speech that legendary Grambling football coach Eddie Robinson delivered to the Little Scholars in attendance. Robinson took time to sign several autographs for fans at the event and later received a gold football for being selected as one of the All-Time Greats of Football. Robinson's success as a coach served as a steppingstone toward the new perception and status of African-American colleges, and he retired from coaching as one of the winningest coaches of all time.

At the VIP Reception, Don Shula, Chuck Bednarik, and Dick Vermeil share a humorous moment. Bednarik (center), an inductee to the Pop Warner Hall of Fame, is considered one of the "last ironmen of football," because he was one of the last professional football players to play an entire game. Bednarik was a seven-time National Football League All-Pro as a linebacker and center for the Philadelphia Eagles.

Yet another sports icon was on hand for the festivities: Gale Sayers, the star running back from the Chicago Bears. Sayers was honored at the event as one of the All-Time Greats of Football, an inductee into the elite Pop Warner Hall of Fame. After retirement from football, Sayers served as the athletic director of Southern Illinois University in Carbondale.

Huddled off to the side, 1979 dinner emcees Tom Brookshier and Jack Whitaker look over the script for the evening ceremony while Randy Grossman and Dick Vermeil look on. Chris Schenkel was scheduled to emcee the event but woke up ill that morning and could not attend. Brookshier and Whitaker rewrote the script a few times, managed to host the event like pros, and received rave reviews for their work.

Irv Cross began the dinner program by welcoming the guests after the national anthem and invocation. Moments later, program chairman Arthur Kaufmann followed Cross by reading the rules of the event. In a humorous moment, Kaufmann threatened to "blow the whistle" and "throw a flag" on anyone who spoke longer than the time allotted for each award. This warning must have worked, because the program ran on schedule throughout the whole night, and Kaufmann was later able to claim, "I told you so."

Prominent Philadelphia attorney Sylvan Cohen represented the Delaware Valley as chairman of the dinner. Here, he announces and welcomes the VIPs that are present for the ceremony, many of whom have traveled from great distances to attend the event. That night alone, Pop Warner guests occupied more than 100 rooms at the Marriot Hotel.

Former CBS Sports employee Jayne Kennedy converses with former Miami Dolphins head coach Don Shula during a break in the evening event. Shula was inducted as an All-Time Great of Football, and Kennedy was on hand to help present several awards throughout the evening, including Mother of the Year and the top scholastically ranked teams. She is shown presenting a National Academic Champion plaque to East Syracuse-Minoa Black Eagles head coach Ken Sheehan.

Helen Dillon, with husband Dr. Tom Dillon (right), talks with Pop Warner board member William S. Fishman, head of ARA Services Inc. Helen Dillon was named the first Pop Warner football Mother of the Year that night for her role with the New York Jets, where she was co-owner of the organization. A Pop Warner Father of the Year award was also presented for several years at the banquet.

Helen Dillon continues to be a dedicated supporter of Pop Warner football and cheerleading. She annually donates money to the national dinner banquet and is also a member of the Pop Warner Little Scholars board of directors. She has lived in Connecticut for several years.

Pop Warner honored 13 people and organizations that played crucial roles in the development of Pop Warner football. The Old Timer's Award was given to, from left to right, Charles Whitacer, representing the Philadelphia Chamber of Commerce; William E. Gillen, managing director of the old Philadelphia Pop Warner Conference following World War II; Andrew Turish, founder for the first professional quality referees organization in Philadelphia; John D. Scott, who was also named Pop Warner's all-time volunteer for his many services; and Joseph Vetter, the first commissioner of record of a Midget football league in the country.

The presentation of the Old Timer's Awards was followed by the entertainment of the Philadelphia Liberty Belles, as they performed various segments of their routines for the guests. Performing "Hot Stuff," from left to right, are Suzan Visco, Nancy Fanslau, and Heidi Malick, the daughter of former Pop Warner treasurer Gordon Malick.

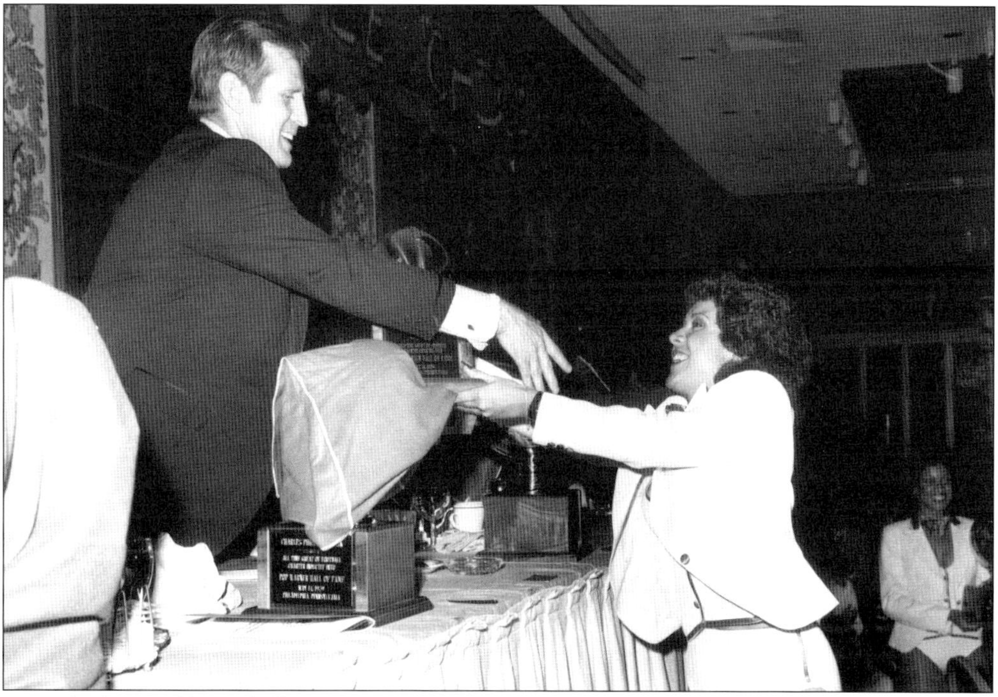

A total of 21 Gold Football Awards were distributed that night to newly enshrined Pop Warner Hall of Fame members for their service to the game of football, as well as to the Pop Warner program specifically. Here, Don Shula and Gale Sayers accept their awards from members of the Philadelphia Liberty Belles. A total of 48 members have been honored with the prestigious award, some of whom include Shula, Vince Lombardi, Dick Butkus, Lynn Swann, Dick Vermeil, Jim Brown, Joseph Tomlin, and Johnny Unitas.

"Pop Warner also teaches youngsters the importance of scholastics. For example, I could not go to football practice 'til my homework was done. So, what it taught me was priorities. That emphasis on education is a discipline that Little Scholars retain for the rest of their lives. I firmly believe that whatever fields of endeavor you might choose to enter . . . business, education, entertainment, community service . . . the lessons you learn in Pop Warner can do nothing but help you in the future," said Joe Theismann, former quarterback for the Washington Redskins.

Five

Pop Warner "Little Scholars"

Scholastics have always been a major part of the Pop Warner program. Founder Joseph Tomlin was a scholar-athlete throughout high school and college, and he emphasized the equal importance of education and athletics. Glenn S. "Pop" Warner, along with Tomlin, attended Harvard Law School and understood the value of education in developing a person's life. In the beginning years of Pop Warner football, the three virtues of participation were considered to be scholarship (40 percent), fellowship (30 percent), and physical fitness (30 percent).

Pop Warner began to identify its top scholar-athletes in the early 1950s. Commonly referred to as the Little Scholars, a select number of participants in the program were honored with this achievement. Oftentimes, the winners would be rewarded with a trip to locations such as New York City or Philadelphia. Here, the 1959 Pop Warner Kids' All-American Team poses for a photograph on the observation roof atop the RCA Building at Rockefeller Center in New York City.

In the early years of the All-American Team of Little Scholars, candidates were judged on a variety of different factors, including schoolwork, extracurricular activities, academic honors and awards, participation in the community, and football skill and other sports participation. Pop Warner still continues to honor student-athletes each year based upon these criteria, and they also use athletic accomplishments as a factor in this process.

Many important people have been strong supporters of Pop Warner because of its emphasis on academics as an equivalent to athletics rather than on athletics alone. Former Georgia governor and U.S. president Jimmy Carter greets the 1972 All-American Team of Little Scholars (below), and former New York State governor Nelson Rockefeller huddles with a team of All-American scholars in New York City (above).

In 1972, Pop Warner started honoring female participants for their academic achievements with the Li'l Miss Pop Warner program. The criteria for selection was similar to the All-American Team of Little Scholars, and a winner was selected each year along with several honorable mention candidates, referred to as her court. Pictured here is the first Li'l Miss Pop Warner recipient, 13-year-old Cynthia Kane of Fairmont, West Virginia.

In an effort to help fund operations of the new national office, Pop Warner Little Scholars held a fundraising dinner. The dinner was a huge success, and a portion of the proceeds was used to bring the 1960 Little Scholars winners to Philadelphia for a three-day trip around the city. The event captured the attention of the city, and support for the program increased. Joseph Tomlin and his staff set out to make this an annual event. Here, the 1960 team of Little Scholars poses for a photograph with Chris Schenkel of CBS Sports, Aileen Mehle of the *New York Daily Mirror*, and Tomlin.

The 1961 team of Little Scholars came to Philadelphia and took a few days to enjoy the sights of the city. Here, they learn about the history of the Liberty Bell, one of the most prominent symbols in America's history. The Little Scholars continued their journey to Europe and the Middle East after departing Philadelphia. The annual trips, called pilgrimages, ended in 1971 due to a lack of funding.

In 1974, prominent Philadelphia industrialist and civic leader Leon Perelman awarded the first Pop Warner scholarship for $1,000. The format was a traditional fishbowl-style selection, in which the winner was selected from a blind draw. The scholarship money was available for each winner to use toward his (only available to boys at the time) first year in college. The scholarship was presented annually by Perelman for six consecutive years.

Philadelphia was a very popular choice amongst the annual pilgrimages of the Little Scholars. In both photographs, the Little Scholars are posing for photographs in front of the statue of Commo. John Barry, which stands on the south side of Independence Hall, the location of the famous Liberty Bell. Philadelphia was an ideal location for the trips not only because of the city's history but also because of its being the home city of the Pop Warner national office.

By the 1988–1989 season, applications for the All-American team had risen to an incredible 3,500, forcing Pop Warner to categorize the recognition by age. That year, 251 participants in the age categories of 9, 10, 11, 12, and "13 years and up," from 13 different states, received the prestigious award. Several of these scholar-athletes gathered below at the annual awards dinner that was held in Philadelphia on May 16, 1988.

For over 50 consecutive years, the Union League of Philadelphia honored young men and women for their citizenship. Nominated yearly by local athletic and youth service organizations, approximately 250 individuals are honored with this award. In this 1988 photograph, Good Citizenship awards are presented by Union League committee member Richard Heuer and Pop Warner employee Jim Taft to, from left to right, Damion Brock, Bruce Malson, and Kelly Sennstorm.

In 1989, after the number of applications eclipsed the 4,000 mark, Pop Warner divided the national scholar winners into five categories based on the students' grade level in school. A total of 35 football players and 15 cheerleaders were selected in each category, the youngest being in third grade and the oldest in the seventh-to-ninth-grade division. The national winners were selected based upon school grades (80 percent) and community-related activities (20 percent). At the annual dinner banquet, the scholars received plaques for their accomplishments, and many took the opportunity to pose for a picture with Lou Holtz, who received the Tomlin Award for his service.

PECO Energy showcased a brilliant lighting display welcoming several Pop Warner Little Scholars to the 1993 National Scholastic All-American Banquet held in Philadelphia. The event took place for several years at the Wyndham Franklin Plaza Hotel in Philadelphia until it was relocated to Disney World in Lake Buena Vista, Florida, in 1995. Disney World has served as host to the National Scholastic All-American Banquet for six of the past nine years.

Although the awarding of scholarships to participants had occurred in years past, it was never a fixture at the annual dinner until 1993. That year, six $1,000 scholarships were awarded on behalf of the Touchdown Club of America to Pop Warner's top scholars. In eight consecutive years of attending the national dinner, the Touchdown Club of America awarded $53,000 in scholarship money to deserving scholar-athletes.

Many companies began to gain interest in rewarding Pop Warner participants for their academic achievements. Proctor & Gamble, Walt Disney World, Xerox Corporation, U.S. Airways, MAC Specialties, and the National Football League Players Association were among those awarding scholarships annually at the national banquet. In 1999, a scholarship fund was also created by the Pop Warner regional directors, awarding two scholarships annually with the money coming directly from the eight Pop Warner regions. Pictured are Reggie Williams of Disney Sports Attractions (above) and Irv Cross of Pop Warner (below) presenting scholarships to deserving students at the 1996 dinner banquet.

In 2002, the National Football League Players Association and Players Inc. made the largest contribution to the Pop Warner Scholarship Fund by donating $20,000 to be used for scholarships at the national banquet. That year, Pop Warner awarded 30 scholarships to deserving scholar-athletes for their academic achievement, with 12 of these scholarships presented on behalf of the National Football League Players Association and Players Inc. Here, top scholar Jazmyn Boulware-Wilburn receives her $5,000 scholarship from 2002 Inspiration to Youth recipient Ricky Williams. The following year, Boulware-Wilburn became the first college student to participate in Pop Warner, at just 13 years old.

Pop Warner held its first official National Awards Recognition program in the spring of 1961. That year, Joe Scott, co-owner of the Philadelphia Flyers, received the first Gold Football Award from Pop Warner Little Scholars. Although the primary purpose was to honor the achievements of prominent businessmen and celebrities, it was the first event that included recognition for scholastic achievement. Several of the Little Scholars were asked to help present the awards to the annual winners.

Six

Pop Warner National Awards Program

Pop Warner began to nationally recognize its volunteers through the Volunteer of the Year Award in 1978, and the award has been given annually ever since at the national banquet. Volunteer of the Year candidates are selected by their peers for dedication to Pop Warner and youth sports. The first recipient of the prestigious award was Jim Hinkle (left), a volunteer from the Stamford, Connecticut, Pop Warner program. At the 1979 awards dinner, Hinkle shares a moment with 1979 Volunteer of the Year recipient Sergio Cisneros.

The Warner Award was established in 1982 by the board of directors of Pop Warner to honor "the person who has achieved academic excellence in athletics, scholarship and life's endeavors, with integrity and humanity." Following Irv Cross and Joseph Tomlin, Miami Dolphins owner Joe Robbie received the third annual award in 1984 in appreciation for all he has done for Pop Warner and football in general. Tomlin looks on from the dais as Robbie receives a warm reception from those in attendance, including Mickey and Goofy. A generous supporter, Robbie began serving as chairman of the Pop Warner board of trustees in 1981 and remained in that position for several years.

Former Washington Redskins' quarterback Joe Theismann donated his support to Pop Warner in many different ways. Theismann began his football days playing for South River Pop Warner in New Jersey. Aside from being an alumnus, he also served as chairman of the Russell Athletic Bowl and always preached the values of scholastics as a part of success in life. Pop Warner rewarded Theismann for his efforts when he was inducted into the Pop Warner Hall of Fame in 1981, with a class that included Dick Butkus, Lynn Swann, and Drew Pearson.

Recipients of Pop Warner awards are selected because they are all outstanding individuals. They have been honored for over 40 years, and they are always willing to stop and sign a few autographs for the fans. Here, dominating linebacker Junior Seau and Hall of Fame wide receiver Lynn Swann take time out to stop and sign footballs for their fans. Oftentimes, the honoree will arrange to hold an autograph session after the event, sometimes staying for over an hour.

The 1993 Pop Warner awards dinner was truly one to remember, as several key people in professional sports were honored for their achievements. Here, National Football League commissioner Paul Tagliabue addresses the audience after receiving the Warner Award. Tagliabue was a National Football League attorney before being elected as the league's fourth commissioner in 1989. During his tenure, Tagliabue has expanded the league from 28 teams to 32 and instituted the salary cap in 1994.

At the 1993 awards dinner, morning honoree Jim Kelly from the Buffalo Bills presented then Minnesota Vikings head coach Dennis Green with the Gold Football Award. While with the Vikings, Green became the winningest coach in the franchise's history, leading the team to eight playoff appearances, including the 1998 season with a 15-1 record, the second-best record of all-time. Trace Armstrong (left) received the Glenn S. Pop Warner Inspiration to Youth Award for his commitment to excellence in the community.

Olympic greatness was also honored at the 1993 celebration, as gold medal winner Donna De Varona became the first female to receive the Tomlin Award, presented to an individual who has demonstrated outstanding character development, physical fitness, and academic achievement. De Varona won gold medals in the 400 individual medley and the 400 freestyle relay at the 1964 Olympics, set 18 world records during her career, and cofounded the Women's Sports Foundation in 1974. The popular Philly Phanatic (right) shares a light moment with a guest.

Warner Award winner Dick Butkus (above right) is honored by Reggie Williams of Disney Sports Attractions in 1995. Butkus, a Hall of Fame linebacker for the Chicago Bears, also runs the Dick Butkus Football Network, a longtime partner and supporter of Pop Warner Little Scholars. Former Denver Broncos running back Terrell Davis (below right), the 1999 Warner Award recipient, is presented with his old Pop Warner football jersey. Davis began his football dominance with Valencia Park Pop Warner in southern California.

In 1996, former Dallas Cowboys running back Emmitt Smith (above left) received more than one honor. With his mother, Mary Smith, looking on, he was presented with the Glenn S. Pop Warner Inspiration to Youth Award for his outstanding service in the community. Presenting the award was Carl Peterson, Pop Warner chairman and Kansas City Chiefs president. What caught Smith off guard, however, was a birthday cake presented to him by Mickey and Minnie Mouse (below). The event was held in Orlando, Florida, on May 25, 1996, just a few days after Smith's 27th birthday.

One of the highlights of the morning Tribute to Scholars Banquet each year is the raffle for prizes. Various companies and National Football League teams and players generously donate items to be raffled off to those scholars who make the trip to Disneyland and Disney World each year. Shown with jerseys that were player donated and autographed are two lucky scholars.

A pair of Pop Warner Hall of Famers, Dick Vermeil (above, inducted in 1986) and Lynn Swann (below, inducted in 1981) are honored for their continued support over the years of the Pop Warner program. Vermeil, head coach of the Kansas City Chiefs and frequent attendee of the Pop Warner awards dinner during his tenure with the Philadelphia Eagles, is rewarded with the Gold Football Award at the 2000 banquet at the Coronado Springs Resort at Walt Disney World. Below, Swann, a National Football League member, receives the Tomlin Award in 2000.

Charles Davis is the longest-running emcee of the Pop Warner awards dinner. Davis, who spent several years with the Sunshine Network in mid-Florida, hosted the event for nearly a decade. The only reason the streak ended was because a new broadcasting job for college football forced him to travel that weekend. Davis's true generosity was apparent when he often presented the money earned for his services as a scholarship to a top scholar-athlete, as shown below in 2002.

Pop Warner cheerleading spokeswoman Paula Abdul was presented with the Female Achievement Award in 2000, becoming just the third recipient of the award. Abdul was also in attendance at Disney's Wide World of Sports for the National Cheer & Dance Championships, where she delivered a powerful greeting to the guests in attendance.

In 1947, the Venango Midgets were led by the first two female coaches in the organization's history. Dixie Casey was the first head coach of the team. In this photograph, assistant coach Chrissy Hornberger lines up the starting offense during a practice. Venango, the closest franchise to Joseph Tomlin's home in Philadelphia, produced many successful teams.

Seven

Key Moments in Pop Warner History

In 1959, the Philadelphia court of common pleas No. 4 issued a nonprofit charter to Pop Warner Little Scholars. The name was selected to underscore the basic concept of Pop Warner; the classroom is as important as the playing field.

In 1959, Walt Disney Studios announced that it would film a two-hour show on Pop Warner football. The show was based on the Pop Warner program in the Los Angeles area, where more than 100 teams were involved in league play. The film, *Moochie of Pop Warner Football,* starred Alan Hale of *Gilligan's Island.* It was a huge success and led to the creation of the Disneyland Bowl in Anaheim, California, which was held annually from 1959 to 1968.

Moochie of Pop Warner Football is also credited with establishing Pop Warner football's mandatory play rule. In the movie, Moochie, described as a cross between Dennis the Menace and an altar boy, was severely uncoordinated and was the reason that mandatory play was invented. At the end of the movie, Moochie scored the touchdown that won his team the Disneyland Bowl.

From Disneyland to Disney World—after 10 consecutive years in Anaheim, California, as the Disneyland Bowl, the Pop Warner national championships relocated to the famous Walt Disney World Resort. Renamed the Walt Disney World Bowl, the new event ran consecutively in Orlando, Florida, from 1969 to 1978. The new home of the event was a huge success, as the players always enjoyed visiting the theme parks after the bowl. Members of various Pop Warner teams pause during a strategy session with top Walt Disney World experts.

Liga Mexicana de Futbol Americano Pop Warner was established in Mexico City in 1963, becoming the first international Pop Warner program in the organization's history. Unfortunately, the first few years saw little progress until Sergio Cisneros took over the program. When just 14 teams were involved, Cisneros stepped in and shaped the organization into a model Pop Warner program. In 1979, Pop Warner Little Scholars honored Cisneros with the Volunteer of the Year Award for all his efforts. By that time, Cisneros was managing 129 teams in his program.

In the summer of 1967, Pop Warner Junior Football League marked its 39th season by adding a new dimension to the program. In an effort to serve youths in every community, the program officially included girls. For the first time in the organization's history, cheerleading squads were recognized as chartered members, and many programs quickly formed.

A gala event is held in the spring of 1979 at the Marriott in Philadelphia to celebrate the golden anniversary of Pop Warner and the charter induction of the Pop Warner Hall of Fame. Former CBS Sports commentator and Philadelphia Eagle Irv Cross chaired the event and the charter induction of the Pop Warner Hall of Fame, which included Vince Lombardi, "Red" Grange, Otto Graham, and Joseph Tomlin. Coaching legend Eddie Robinson and former Redskins quarterback Sunny Jurgensen (above) converse after being inducted into the inaugural class. Cross presents the scholastic award to Li'l Miss Pop Warner recipient Donna Loper (left) the first year scholars receive their awards at the annual banquet.

In 1983, in response to many requests, a flag football program was initiated. Originally designed for teams on a tight budget, the sport has become an excellent training ground for tackle leagues. In its inception year, flag programs were established in Connecticut, Florida, Michigan, Missouri, Pennsylvania, Texas, and Mexico. Flag programs had many benefits, including low-cost insurance and optional postseason tournaments. Also, flag football was played during the tackle program's off-season.

From 1983 to 1985, the Pop Warner national championships took place in Alexander City, Alabama. Named the Russell Athletic Bowl due to its main sponsor, Russell Athletics, the event featured teams from three Pop Warner Divisions: Pee Wee, Junior Midget, and Midget. The participating teams, however, were selected by a comprehensive playoff system based on athletic and academic achievements, taking into consideration win-loss records as well as grade point averages for each team. The event was also commonly referred to as Super Bowl Saturday.

England joined the ranks of the Pop Warner football program in 1986 by established a flag football program. Based in Swindon, in Wiltshire, the program was called the Step Achievement League. The organization's founder, Simon O'Hara, used his great knowledge of American football to help form the league and spread the word of Pop Warner across the United Kingdom. That same year, 10 new domestic flag programs were formed in the United States.

In 1988, Pop Warner football and cheerleading once again chartered new waters overseas, this time in Japan. Based in Osaka, the new Japanese Pop Warner Conference (above) was named the Chestnut League. Pictured are scenes from one of the very first games to take place in the Chestnut League, a program that remains intact today. Just nine years later, the Moscow Patriots formed and became the first Pop Warner association in Russia.

In 1988, Pop Warner took a giant step toward enhancing its cheerleading program, adding a national cheerleading competition for squads nationwide. In the Atlanta suburb of Doraville, Georgia, 35 cheer squads in the Junior Pee Wee, Pee Wee, Junior Midget, Midget, and Senior Midget divisions performed their best two routines in front of a panel of expert judges. In a show of appreciation for the new event, each squad was introduced and warmly welcomed during corresponding football games that weekend.

In 1995, the Pop Warner national championships moved to a new home at the Walt Disney World Resort in Lake Buena Vista, Florida. The 1995 National Cheer & Dance Championships were held that year on Walt Disney World property at MGM Studios. The Pop Warner Super Bowl began on property at the then brand-new Disney's Wide World of Sports Complex just two years later. The 1995 Junior Pee Wee Dance champions (below) from Jackson, New Jersey, pose for their team picture after winning the title.

In 1997, Pop Warner took part in celebrating the inaugural year of Disney's Wide World of Sports Complex in Lake Buena Vista, Florida, by holding its national championships at the new facilities. The football championships, known as the Pop Warner Super Bowl, took place throughout the week-long event on four brand-new multipurpose fields, equipped with lighting and nearly flawless grass. The National Cheer & Dance Championships were held indoors in what is now known as the Milk House, which featured stadium seating that was routinely filled for the event. Disney's Wide World of Sports was now the new home of the event.

In 1999, another Pop Warner first occurred when a Midget football team from Jacksonville, Florida, traveled overseas to participate in the first ever international competition, a goodwill exchange against the Moscow Patriots in Russia. The game, named the Friendship Bowl, took place in Moscow in front a large crowd during the third year of the Russian program. The Friendship Bowl continued for several years, the last coming at the 2002 Pop Warner Super Bowl.

One of the highlights of the 2003 Pop Warner Super Bowl and National Cheer & Dance Championships was the grand opening of the new Walt Disney World Resort hotel Pop Century. The Junior Pee Wee team from Naperville, Illinois, which competed the previous day, was invited to help kick off the festivities. Here, the team poses in front of the new property, which is a theme-styled resort featuring games and amenities for all types of vacationers.

On September 11, 2002, just one year after terrorist attacks on New York City and Washington, D.C., Pres. George W. Bush took time to greet several Pop Warner youngsters on the lawn at the White House in the nation's capital. Before leaving for several National Football League opening games that weekend, Bush met with Pop Warner players from Washington-area teams and wished them good luck on their upcoming season.

Pop Warner history is made by 11-year-old Jasmine Plummer of the Harvey Colts in Chicago, Illinois. Plummer became the first female quarterback in the history of Pop Warner to participate in the national championships. The Colts lost their opening-round game to the Southeast Apaches of Texas 13-2, but bounced back to defeat the Kailua Mustangs of Hawaii 14-0 in the consolation game, as Plummer scored the opening touchdown of the game. Plummer's participation sparked the interest of such media moguls as ESPN, Fox Sports, Sports Illustrated, and CNN, all of which ran features on the remarkable young player. (Above and below courtesy Cy Jariz Cyr, *Kickoff Magazine*.)

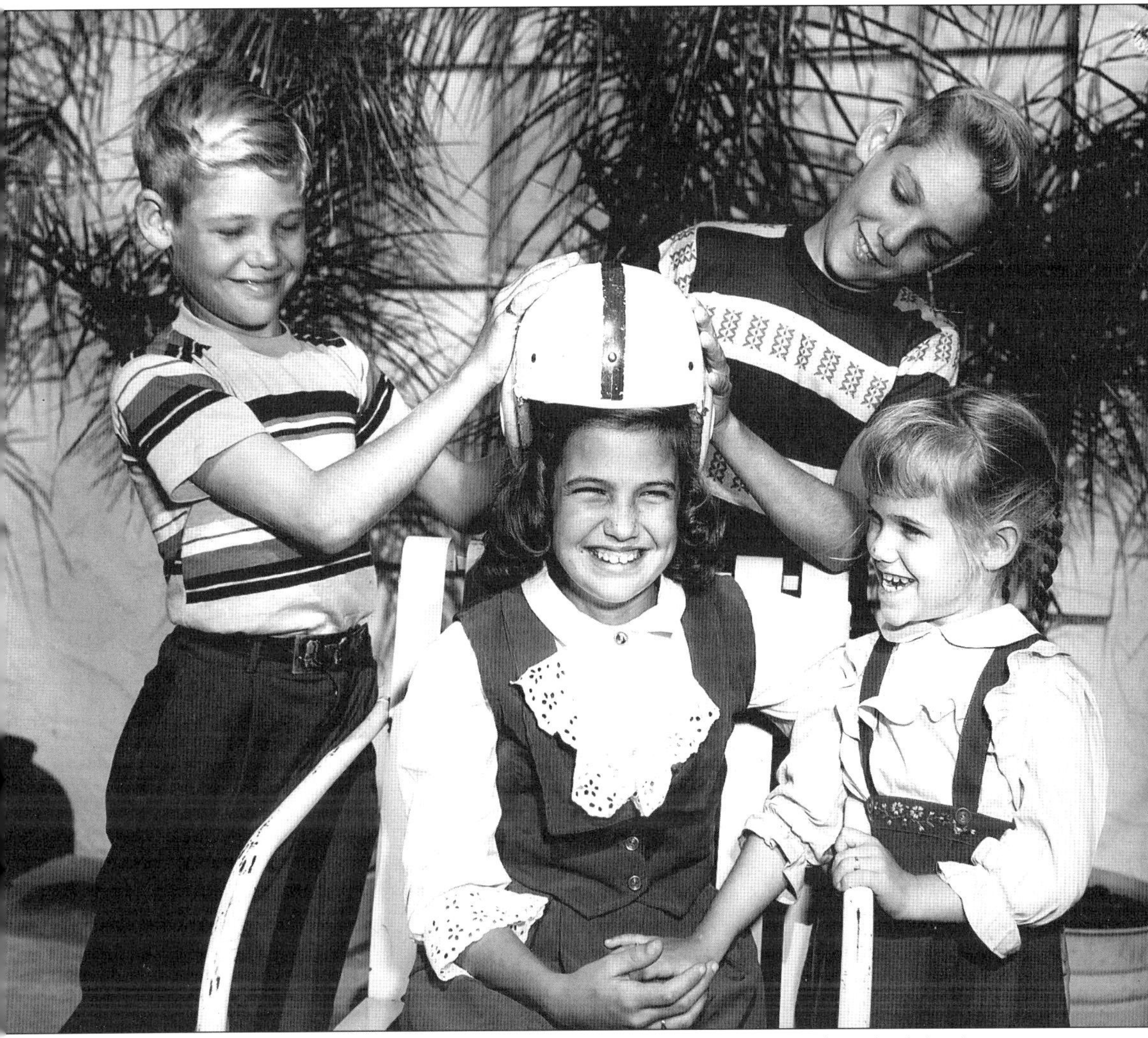

Although Jasmine Plummer's participation in the Pop Warner Super Bowl marked the first year a female had played quarterback for her team, girls had been allowed to play tackle football in the Pop Warner program for many years. However, it was not until the early 21st century that female participation really began to rise steadily and accounted for approximately one percent of the total number of tackle football players in Pop Warner football.

Participants in the Pop Warner spirit program (cheerleading and dance) compete in one of several different divisions of play. Squads are broken down by age into divisions such as Pee Wee and Midget, competing as a large or small squad depending on the number of participants, with a maximum of 35. Squads can also compete in the traditional category, meaning they perform during the standard Pop Warner season, or in the year-round category.

Eight

Pop Warner Today

The participants in the Pop Warner cheer and dance program are unique compared to those of other youth programs. While they are taught about the values of competition, they are also maintaining their grades at a satisfactory level in order to participate.

The end of the 20th century and beginning of the 21st century have seen an explosion in the numbers of participants in cheerleading and dance, especially in Pop Warner. In the early 1990s, there were some 3,000 Pop Warner cheerleading programs in the country. By 2002, that number had reached nearly 5,000. Today, with 150,000 participants, the program accounts for 40 percent of all Pop Warner teams.

Due to the program's popularity and growth, Pop Warner has worked hard to keep pace with the many new changes in the cheer and dance industry. A standard set of rules has been enforced to ensure a fair, safe, and balanced environment for all participants, regardless of squad size or division. These rules are strictly enforced throughout the season. One particular rule unique to Pop Warner disallows tryouts of any kind, leaving anyone interested in participating free to do so.

Anyone who thinks that cheerleading is strictly a sideline sport has never attended a competition. Whether it is a local, regional, or national event, the hard work, dedication, and camaraderie of a Pop Warner cheerleading squad is obvious. Intense practice and discipline are what set squads apart from one another. During a typical competition, a squad is evaluated on its best 2-minute-and-30-second performance, and the championship often hinges on a slight bobble or improper movement.

The Pop Warner program has always valued the importance of offering several camps and clinics to all of its participants. In the past few years, Pop Warner has teamed up with cheerleading mogul National Cheerleaders Association (NCA) to provide camps across the country. The "mega-camps," as they are commonly called, typically run for at least two days, teach each individual the latest in industry standards, and stress the importance of simply having fun. Pictured are two Pop Warner-NCA mega-camps in the summer of 2003.

A cheerleading squad from Moscow, Russia, flew with its football team to Walt Disney World to take part in the 2002 Pop Warner National Cheer & Dance Championships. The squad cheered as the Russian football team played in the annual Friendship Bowl against a Pop Warner team from nearby Orlando, Florida. When the 15 Russian cheerleaders performed their stellar routine for the championships, they amazed the sold-out crowd and later received a commemorative plaque for their participation.

The annual Pop Warner National Cheer & Dance Championships have blossomed from just a few squads competing against one another to a two-day event featuring nearly 200 squads, all competing for the ultimate prize of being crowned national champion. The event, which takes place in the Milk House at Disney's Wide World of Sports Complex, features several squads from each of Pop Warner's eight regions. In order for squads to advance to the national championships, they must win their respective league and regional competition, which take place in the weeks preceding the event.

The year 2002 marked the first year of the Pop Warner National Cheerleading Invitational competition. The event was established to coincide with the vast growth of the cheerleading program, evident throughout the regional championships. Some 65 squads compete in the two-day event, with a winner being selected in four age categories. Each first-place squad also earns a spot in the Pop Warner national cheerleading championships, which are held just a few days later.

The competitions crown outright champions in each division of play, but Pop Warner also recognizes squads that have shown superior teamwork, friendship, and sportsmanship throughout the event. Each year, one squad is selected in each age division for both cheerleading and dance as the recipient of the Spirit of Sportsmanship Award. Squads are observed off the competition floor and their behavior is judged according to what model representatives of Pop Warner cheer and dance should be.

The Pop Warner cheer and dance program has come full circle from the early days of the program. New programs are sprouting up across the country, all wanting to be part of the new phenomenon in youth sports. The program encourages youth participation, ensures safe and positive playing environments, and instills lifelong values of teamwork, dedication, and work ethics in the classroom and in competition. These objectives contribute to the Pop Warner spirit program's position as the largest youth program of its kind in the country.

Pop Warner is the only youth sports organization that requires satisfactory performance in the classroom to participate. The young boys and girls who take part in the program each year are taught the values of education as equivalent to those of athletics. The only individual recognition in Pop Warner is the selection of a National Scholar All-American Team, composed of the top one percent of participants based on school grades and academic and community-related achievements. Today, over 4,000 youngsters are honored with this prestigious recognition, a tradition that began in 1951.

The National Scholar Recognition Banquet is held annually to honor the recipients of the Scholar All-American program. The two-part event takes place over Memorial Day weekend. At the morning tribute, each scholar receives a certificate of achievement, guest speakers address the attendees, and a raffle of donated items takes place. At the evening banquet, sports figures and Volunteers of the Year are honored for their service and scholarships are presented to the top scholars. Since 1993, over $250,000 has been presented to 176 boys and girls in the Pop Warner program.

Today, there are over 6,000 tackle football and 900 flag football teams participating in the Pop Warner football program. Some 210,000 young men and women from 42 states take part in the program during the season that runs from August to December, including the postseason. Each team operates under a uniform set of rules. Strictly enforced, these rules were drafted to resemble the National Federation of State High School Association's national rules.

Safety is the number-one priority in Pop Warner football. A strict age-weight matrix is followed by all participating teams to promote fair competition and to reduce the risk and reality of injuries. In fact, the injury rate in Pop Warner football is less than one-third of that in high-school football, less than one-fifth of that in college football, and less than one-ninth of that in professional football. In a study done by the U.S. Consumer Product Safety Commission, it was found that organized football among 5- to 15-year-olds has 12 percent fewer injuries per capita than organized soccer, 50 percent fewer injuries per capita than bicycle riding, and 74 percent fewer injuries per capita than skateboarding.

The Pop Warner Super Bowl features the top 64 teams from four age-weight divisions competing for a national title in division one and division two. Every year, one team in each division represents one of the eight Pop Warner football regions and competes in the annual event at Disney's Wide World of Sports Complex in Lake Buena Vista, Florida. Pop Warner is the only youth football organization with a true national championship game.

Each year, the division one Midget national championship game is featured on an hourlong special produced by National Football League Films. The special is aired on ESPN and ESPN2 throughout the month of January, leading up to the National Football League Super Bowl. Players of the Marshall Heights Bison (above) make their way onto the field before the 2003 national championship game against the Dale City Cowboys from northern Virginia. From Washington, D.C., the Bison team has participated in this game three different years beginning in the late 1990s.

One of the greatest games ever played in the Pop Warner Super Bowl took place in 2002, when the Northwood Rams from Maryland defeated the Alaska South Central Eagles from northern Alaska by the score of 24-18 in a triple-overtime thriller. After the game, Rams head coach Herb Estep (left) and Eagles head coach Larry Jackson answer a few questions for the ESPN television special. Estep led the Rams to consecutive national championships in 2001 and 2002.

The road to the Pop Warner Super Bowl is a long one for the football players. First, in order to be eligible for participation, each player must pass a medical examination, provide proof of academic fitness, and have parental consent before the season begins. Players start preparing for the seven- to nine-game season schedule on August 1. Top teams in each division move on to league, state, and regional competition, en route to the Pop Warner Super Bowl.

The Pop Warner Super Bowl was first held at Disney's Wide World of Sports Complex in 1997, the inaugural season of the sports complex. Since then, it has become a staple at the sports complex, which offers all the transportation, lodging, and athletic facilities necessary to host the event. Overlooking the four football fields is a commemorative plaque (below), given to Pop Warner Little Scholars in the late 1990s by Walt Disney World in appreciation of the event.

The National Football League Players Association estimates that between 60 and 70 percent of National Football League players began their careers participating in Pop Warner football. An impressive alumni list is highlighted by the likes of Ricky Williams, Eddie George, Joe Theismann, Joe Montana, Lynn Swann, and Terrell Davis, among others. Current National Football League commissioner Paul Tagliabue once said, "Pop Warner is really important because you have kids trying to determine what their values are, what their priorities in life are, and what their vision in life is going to be."

Participation in the Pop Warner program offers many advantages. Pop Warner clinics and programs are held throughout the country, with subjects ranging from safety issues, equipment, and tips to drills for improving knowledge of the game. Each team is required to meet national insurance standards, the best insurance programs in American youth sports. Also, with school budgets often eliminating extracurricular activities, Pop Warner is becoming an ally to local school and recreation programs.

Above all else, participation, teamwork, and dedication are ingrained into each individual who participates in the program, on and off the playing field. None of this would be possible, however, without the dedicated leaders and personnel who guide the program. Pop Warner has over 37,000 coaches and one million parents, fans, and volunteers who take an active part in the lives of Pop Warner youth. Without their endless support and generosity, the program would cease to exist.

As Pop Warner Little Scholars marks its 75th year anniversary, the roots and history of the organization will be celebrated. The program started back in 1929 as the idea of a dedicated young sports enthusiast named Joseph Tomlin and evolved around a football coaching legend named Pop Warner. A four-team conference in Philadelphia blossomed into what today is a worldwide program for young people ages 5 to 16. No matter what the year, however, the mission of Pop Warner Little Scholars remains the same: within a safe and structured environment, enabling children to benefit from participation in team sports, teaching fundamental values, skills, and knowledge that they can use throughout their lives.